Francis Dobbs

The Patriot King

Francis Dobbs

The Patriot King

ISBN/EAN: 9783744713641

Printed in Europe, USA, Canada, Australia, Japan

Cover: Foto ©ninafisch / pixelio.de

More available books at **www.hansebooks.com**

Francis Dobbs

The Patriot King

ISBN/EAN: 9783744713641

Printed in Europe, USA, Canada, Australia, Japan

Cover: Foto ©ninafisch / pixelio.de

More available books at **www.hansebooks.com**

THE

PATRIOT KING;

OR

IRISH CHIEF.

A

TRAGEDY.

Performed at the THEATRE in SMOCK-
ALLEY, DUBLIN.

By FRANCIS DOBBS.

The Countess of ELY.

Madam,

ENCOURAGED by the readiness with which you patronised the IRISH CHIEF, when represented on the *Dublin* Stage, I have ventured to offer that performance to the world, under the sanction of your Ladyship's name. I hope you will pardon the liberty I have taken in doing so, without first obtaining your permission. I should not have presumed so far, had not your Ladyship been pleased to express your approbation of my play, when I had the honour of laying it before you at *Rathfarnham*.

I am

I am convinced it would be highly disagreeable to you, were I to purfue the common mode of Dedications: I shall therefore refrain from a subject, on which I could with pleasure expatiate; and shall only beg leave to assure you, that I am, with the greatest respect,

Your Ladyship's Most devoted

And most grateful humble Servant,

FRANCIS DOBBS.

ADVER-

ADVERTISEMENT.

IT may not be unneceſſary to acquaint the Reader, that this piece was performed in Dublin, at Smock-Alley Theatre, in April 1773.

The Author thought, from his obſervations during the performance, that many uſeful alterations, omiſſions, and additions might be made; and he flatters himſelf that he has much improved his play ſince that period.

The character of Cleones is entirely new, and of courſe the ſcenes between him and Pharon (formerly Tor;) whoſe paſſion for Stira is alſo an addition.

The cataſtrophe of this Tragedy was formerly unhappy, as Stira was really poiſoned: the Author, however, hath yielded to the opinion of his friends, and has given a more fortunate concluſion.

The ingenious Mr. Melmoth, who filled the character of Ceallachan, made many judicious alterations in that part; but, as the Author cannot think of offering any thing in print to the public that is not

moſt

moſt ſtrictly his own, he has entirely omitted them ; and chooſes rather to want the ornaments of Mr. Melmoth's pen, than ſhine with borrowed luſtre.

The Author once had the higheſt ambition of being the compoſer of a well-received Tragedy : led away by youth and inexperience, he vainly hoped to ſucceed in his wiſhes, and, at the age of twenty-one, he firſt wrote the IRISH CHIEF. Time, however, hath ſince ſhown him his error, and he hath for ever relinquiſhed the idle expectation of Poetic Fame.

The Author of this piece will not be ſo illiberal as to rail at the Managers : his play has, without doubt, a thouſand imperfections, and perhaps a much greater number than are ſufficient to juſtify its rejection from the Theatres of Covent-Garden and Drury-lane : the Public, however, have ſometimes differed from the opinion even of a Mr. Garrick or a Mr. Coleman ; and it is not impoſſible but they may allow as much merit to the IRISH CHIEF, as to a *Chriſtmas Tale*, an *Iriſh Widow*, or, a *Man of Buſineſs*.

PRO-

Written by the AUTHOR:

To be fpoken in the Character of CEALLACHAN.

HEAR me, ye Beaus: ye Critics, hear me too:
  By me, the Author humbly fues to you:
Requefts your favour in his pending caufe;
And from your kindnefs only, hopes applaufe.
That managers have furer means, we know—
Our Bard, alas! no orders can beflow.

  'Midft many dangers, many dreadful fears,
One gleam of hope the affrighted Poet chears.
It muft be granted that his piece is new;
And novelty, 'tis faid, you all purfue.

  Full oft hath honeft Teague been here difplay'd;
And many a roar have Irifh blunders made:
The bull, the brogue, are now fo common grown;
That one would almoft fwear they were—your own.
But, lo! to-night, what you ne'er faw before,
A tragic hero from Hibernia's fhore;
Who fpeaks as you do, both of men and things;
And talks heroics, juft like other kings.

  Irifh heroics! yonder Cit exclaims!
Who's been to Hackney, and has crofs'd the Thames:
Who forms his judgment from a few dull plays,
And thinks a Porter's, is a nation's phrafe.

  To hold forth Nature, once the Stage was meant:
'Tis ftrangely alter'd from its firft intent.
Were we by it to judge Ierne's fons,
They all are honeft—but they all are clowns.
Yet truth hath faid, and I fhall take her word,
That fome have grac'd a court—and fome a cord.

  Know ye what part I act, who fpeak fo well?
I'd lay my life not one in ten can tell:
So many lines without an Irifh howl,
Without by Jafus, or upon my fhoul:
'Tis ftrange indeed—nor can I hope belief,
When I declare myfelf, the IRISH CHIEF.

B

DRAMATIS PERSONÆ.

CEALLACHAN, King of Munster, in love with STIRA,   Mr. MELMOTH.

DUNCAN, Friend to Ceallachan,   Mr. WILMOT.

SITRICK, Chief of the Danes in Ireland, and a Prince of the royal blood of Denmark,   Mr. SPARKS, jun.

PHARON, General to Sitrick, in love with Stira alfo,   Mr. KANE.

CLEONES, Friend to Pharon,   ————

BEDA, Wife to Sitrick, fecretly in love with Ceallachan,   Mrs. T. BARRY.

STIRA, Sifter to Sitrick, and in love with Ceallachan alfo,   Mrs. SPARKS.

OFFICERS, GUARDS, ATTENDANTS, &c.

SCENE, *DUBLIN, and the Country adjacent.*

THE
PATRIOT KING, &c.

ACT I.

SCENE, *Palace of* Dublin.

STIRA, BEDA.

STIRA.

AT length, my Beda, is the time arriv'd,
 When anxious doubts and fears shall be no more.
The great Ceallachan this morning comes,
Comes to bestow felicity supreme.
Not even Hope, with all her flatt'ring train,
Had promis'd to my wishes such success.

BEDA.

His virtues well I know, and own indeed,
His worth unrivall'd sends its lustre forth:
Yet still 'tis strange that Sitrick should unite,

To

To Denmark's royal line, its greateft foe.
What will each fubject fay, when they behold
Him who hath fpilt their deareft kindred's blood,
Thus honour'd by our chief---and thus efpous'd?---

S T I R A.

The Danes to virtue are not yet fo loft,
But they will give that praife his actions claim ;
Nor can they blame the conduct that deftroy'd---
No wanton quarrel urg'd him to the war :
To fave his country from the Danifh yoke
He drew his fword ; and by his conqu'ring arm,
At once fecur'd its freedom, and his crown.
Sitrick fhould rather have his people's thanks
For making thus a deadly foe their friend,
Who ftill hath brought difhonour on their arms,
And fent them vanquifh'd from the field of death.

B E D A.

E'en fhould the Danes thefe look'd-for rites approve,
Hath e'er this hero giv'n one proof of love ?
Seldom do princes from affection wed ;
To politics they oft muft yield their choice.
Perhaps his people, tir'd of blood and war,
Requeft him to accept thy offer'd hand,
And thus reftore them to the fweets of peace---
What then can Stira hope but cold refpect ?---
Will cold refpect repay a flame like thine ?

S T I R A.

O Beda ! do not thus difturb my mind,
Nor raife up thoughts that would for ever blaft
My promis'd harveft of unequall'd blifs ---
Did I not think his heart beat high with love,

Did

Did I not think that heart was wholly mine,
This hand fhould fooner end my hated life,
Than at the altar join Ceallachan's.---

B E D A.

Why then thefe hafty nuptials thus approve,
Whilft e'en fufpicion can afford a doubt?---

S T I R A.

Why fhould I doubt? Do I not know he loves?
His eyes, thofe true revealers of the foul,
Have oft-times told me what his tongue with-held;
Each little act was with attention drefs'd,
And ev'ry look his tendernefs proclaim'd...
This is the language of a lover's heart,
This is the language that can ne'er deceive---

B E D A.

The mind that kindly feels for others woes,
With looks of foftnefs pours its ready balm,
And fteals affliction from the eye of forrow:
When firft ye met, you were a captive maid;
Impute not falfely to the pow'r of love,
What gen'rous pity might as well produce.

S T I R A.

Oh, no! tho' pity in a heart like his,
Muft fympathife with ev'ry wretch's woe;
That foft regard which cannot be exprefs'd,
Nor yet mifunderftood, muft wanting be;
To mutual paffion it is only known,
And none but thofe who feel its pow'r believe.

Enter

Enter an Attendant to STIRA.

ATTENDANT.

Madam, a chief arriv'd from Munſter's king
Requeſts admittance.

S T I R A.

Go bid him enter. [*Exit Attend.*
O my lov'd friend, a thouſand fears ariſe---
But, lo ! the valiant Duncan hither com es ;
Than him, none nearer to his monarchs thoughts---

Enter D U N C A N.

Moſt welcome, Sir---

B E D A.

Moſt welcome to theſe walls---
How fares the king ? Doth he ſtill his purpoſe hold ?
Hath ought prevented his intended ſpeed?

D U N C A N.

Madam, the king with fondeſt ardour burns,
To meet his deſtin'd bride---one hour from hence,
He with impatience waits for my return.
Mean time, ſome ſecret thoughts for her I bear,
Whom ſoon I hope to call my queen.----

S T I R A.

Speak out.
Whate'er it is, 'tis ſafe in Beda's breaſt.----

D U N C A N.

This morn retir'd beneath a ſhady bow'r,
My royal Lord in terms like theſe, addreſs'd
Mine ear---Go tell the lovely fair, he ſaid,

Whoſe

Whofe charms unrivall'd rule thy monarch's heart,
That fhe alone can happinefs beftow ;
Can give that blifs, which crowns might feek to buy,
Yet find the purchafe far beyond their reach.
But, oh ! my Duncan, tell the beauteous maid,
If in her breaft a dearer object lives,
Or fhould a brother's will her hand direct
Where inclination doth not prompt its courfe----
Oh ! tell her, I refign thefe promis'd rites,
And fingly wretched to my throne return.----

STIRA.

Go tell the gen'rous prince from whom you came,
(For Stira's foul difdains her fex's arts)
That ev'ry future blifs on him depends---
Tell him, without a blufh I own my love,
And view with rapture the approaching hour,
That makes me ever his.----

DUNCAN.

           ---Oh ! heavenly founds ;
Thus let me to my gracious princefs kneel,
And on her hand my faithful homage pay.----
Now to th' impatient king I'll quickly fly ;
And give a tranfport never felt before.   [*Exit.*

STIRA.

Each doubting thought begone---with equal flame
His bofom glows, and Stira is moft blefs'd --
In pleafing tranfport ev'ry nerve is wrap'd---
My heart as if impatient to take flight,
And fpring to where its wifhes long have been,
Is fcarce contain'd in this, its little cell---
Beda forgive the raptures of a lover---

Some

Some ordinary cares demand me now ;
This morning paſt, love claims each future hour.---

[Exit.

Manet B E D A.

To one unpractis'd in deceit, how hard
To wear a ſmile whilſt daggers pierce the heart,
And ſeem delighted with what wounds it moſt.
Theſe nuptials make a wretch of me indeed.---
Sure happineſs can ne'er that boſom fill,
Where paſſion prompts, what honor muſt forbid---
This king belov'd by me, by Sitrick's wife,
Now haſtes to wed the ſiſter of my lord---
Diſtraction!---what!---am I then doom'd to ſee
The man my heart adores, another's---No---
That, that, I cannot bear.---I'll to my huſband,
With Daniſh pride inflame his haughty ſoul,
And ſtop theſe rites, ſo fatal to my peace.   [Exit.

S C E N E changes to a different Part of
Dublin.

Enter P H A R O N and C L E O N E S.

P H A R O N.

O my Cleones, I knew not till this hour,
The wondrous height my paſſion hath attain'd :
The beauteous Stira mingles with each wiſh,
Beats in each pulſe, and throbs thro' ev'ry vein :
---And ſhall this day beſtow her on another ?
Firſt ſhall this hand implant a dagger here,
Or ſheath one in the heart of Munſter's king.

C L E O.

CLEONES.

What madnefs doth poffefs thy heated mind?
This Stira never can be thine---even grant
Ceallachan thefe nuptials had refus'd ;
What hopes for thee remain'd?---Sitrick, thou know'ft,
Beholds even kings with fcorn ;---fo high he rates
The ancient honours of his royal line.

PHARON.

Where is the mighty merit to defcend
From kings, who trace their boafted anceftry
Even from the fabled Deities of Heav'n?
Flows there a richer current thro' the veins?
Pants in the breaft a more exalted worth?
Doth clay ennobled, purify the foul;
Or give a virtue humbler birth denies?---

CLEONES.

No, Pharon ; but the world is here the judge ;
We may condemn, not alter its decree.
Yet fay, had Fortune been a kinder dame,
How would the beauteous Stira be difpofed?
Doth fhe behold thee with a partial eye,
And blufh compliance on thy wifhes?

PHARON.

---Alas!
No tender glance hath e'er allay'd my pain,
No fweet confufion blufh'd a kind confent ;
Yet do I love her to that pitch of frenzy,
She muft, fhe fhall be mine---

CLEONES.

---She muft be yours!---
O impotence of paffion !---Doth not this hour,
C   This

This very hour, beftow her on another,
And blaft thy foolifh hopes for ever?---

PHARON.

      ---This hour,
If Fortune favours, gives her to my arms---
For know, my friend, e'en now the ready bark
Unfurls her canvafs to the coming winds,
Spreads every fail to catch the precious breeze,
And waft us from Ierne's fhore---

CLEONES.

      ---What then
Can Pharon ftoop, thus meanly to poffefs
The injur'd form of weeping innocence?---
Think'ft thou Love's holy raptures can be thine?
When, not the foft murmurs of the yielding maid,
Nor yet the fweet refiftance beauty gives,
But tears and harfh complaints affail thine ear,
Pierce thro' thy heart, and load thee with remorfe:
Then Pharon wilt thou curfe this hateful day,
And damn that hour which gave thee being---

PHARON.

      ---O ftop---
Recall not feelings that were lull'd to reft;
But lend thy aid to bear the fair one hence:
Let Pharon clafp this charmer to his breaft,
And revel in ecftatic fcenes of blifs.

CLEONES.

 Such are indeed the fcenes of mutual love---
When the fond female in each look declares
The rifing tumults of a foft defire:
When, fearful of fenfations yet unknown,

           The

The blufhing maid with downcaft eye confents,
And trembling fills a lover's arms---then, then
Indeed, to clafp her to the panting breaft,
To foothe with all the eloquence of love,
And drive thofe idle fears away---is blifs,
Is ecftacy divine !---But you, my Lord,
Oh! what have you to hope ?---you---

PHARON.

      ---Cleones ceafe---

At once declare there's danger in the tafk
That Friendfhip hath requir'd ; nor meanly feek
To hide thy fears beneath the veil of honour.--

CLEONES.

 You are unkind, my Lord; I might fay more:
Where obligations bind the heart, the obliger
Should be more delicate---

PHARON.

      ---And the obliged
More grateful.---

CLEONES.

    ---More grateful cannot be---
Had you but bade me rufh on certain death,
You fhould have feen how little life was priz'd.
My honour is, I own, a dearer ftake ;
Nor can ev'n gratitude oblige Cleones
To part with virtue.---

PHARON.

   ---This wond'rous virtue too
No doubt will make thee hafte to Sitrick's prefence,
And all my fcheme betray.---

CLEONES.

---Fear not, my Lord :
You fpoke in friendſhip, as a friend I heard.
So facred is fuch converſe held by me,
That racks and tortures ſhould extort in vain.
The poſt, which, by your favour was obtain'd,
I here refign---And now, my Lord, farewell---
You'll eafy find a more obſequious friend ;
A truer is perhaps beyond your reach.

[*Exit.*

Manet PHARON.   I

Oh! thou haſt touch'd me to the very foul,
Made me examine this my purpos'd deed,
And ſtruck a horror o'er the confcious mind :
The very crime with which I raſhly charg'd thee
Rebounds upon myſelf---by Sitrick's power,
Plac'd in the firſt high office of the ſtate,
I feek to bear his lovely fiſter hence,
And thus repay the bounteous hand that rais'd me.
Oh! I ſhall feek thee my Cleones,
Fall on thy neck, and wet thee with my tears,
Till thou, relenting, feel foft pity rife,
And giv'ſt a pardon to repenting folly ;
Then wilt thou teach me to regain repofe,
And conquer paſſion, by the force of honour.

[*Exit.*

Enter SITRICK, BEDA.

Scene changes to the Palace.

BEDA.

Worthlefs would be the partner of thy bed,
If ſhe concealed ought affecting thee.

The

The people murmur, and with loud outcry
Declare their hatred of thefe purpos'd rites.
Shall he, they fay, whofe fword fo oft hath reek'd
With fathers', brothers', and with kinfmens' gore,
Now light the nuptial torch amidft our grief!
Much more than this, they publicly declare:
Should Sitrick ftill perfift, Oh! who can tell
Where fuch repinings end!---

SITRICK.

          ---Thanks to thy love;
But Sitrick fears no danger from fuch threats.
E'er yet to-morrow bids the world adieu,
Their praife, not cenfure, fhall my zeal reward.

BEDA.

  Truft not, my Lord, to fuch uncertain hopes,
Nor think to lead the mean, ignoble crowd,
By Reafon's force. In vain doth wifdom try
To calm their paffions, and their wrath reftrain:
When thoughtlefs fury fpurs, away they run,
And ev'ry ftep leaves judgment more behind.

SITRICK.

  Fear not the prudent conduct of thy Lord;
Well fkill'd, I hold the reins of fov'reign pow'r,
Know when to treat men with an eafy hand,
And how to curb them in their mad career.

BEDA.

  But grant thy people fhould their rage refign:
Can Sitrick ftoop to join his royal houfe
To Munfter's petty king?---Where now that pride,
Which once infpir'd the bofom of my lord?---
Haft thou forgiv'n that hand, fo oft uprear'd,

To pluck the laurel from thy brow, to blaft
Thy glory,. and o'erturn each conqueft paft,
By prefent fhame and deep difgrace.---

SITRICK.

---Forgiv'n !
But little doft thou know the foul of Sitrick---
Vengeance alone, for wrongs like mine, atone.---

BEDA.

And as a proof of which, you feek to give
A fifter to his arms!---

SITRICK.

---Well may'ft thou fcorn
The feeming bafenefs.   Yet know, my Beda,
Such muft the glorious fequel be, that you,
Even you, fhall give applaufe.---

BEDA.

---What ? fhall I praife
The timorous dictates of a poor difmay ?
Prudence perhaps may juftify the deed ;
Perhaps the beauteous Stira may perfuade
This conquering monarch to with-hold his arms,
And fpare the timid Dane.---

SITRICK.

---Nay, taunt not thus---
The Danes no more fhall feel his power---e'en now
Doth Munfter totter on the verge of ruin ;
And all her laurels fade, to bloom no more.---

BEDA.

Ha ! what fay'ft thou ? explain thy doubtful words ?
SITRICK.

SITRICK.

The event my hidden meaning shall unfold.---

BEDA.

I pr'ythee, Sitrick, indulge my curious ear,
And let thy secret purpose be reveal'd.---

SITRICK.

Farewell---I know thy sex's weakness better---
Eager to hear, impatient to reveal;
Give but a secret to the breast of woman,
Some fav'rite female shares the sacred trust,
Who to another must disclose it too;
Till thus, 'tis whisper'd o'er a prying world. [*Exit.*

Manet BEDA.

Thoughts rush upon me, that increase, not heal
The wounds within my breast---Some dark design,
Some deep-laid stratagem my fears display,
Full of destruction to th' Hibernian king;
Whose open unsuspicious soul, ne'er thought
Of deeds in others which himself abhor'd.---
Sitrick is subtle, cruel, and so dead
To all the finer feelings of the mind,
Where honour dwells,---that virtue in a foe,
But heightens and inflames his rage.----Ah, why!
Allur'd by title and the farce of state,
Will woman throw her happiness away?
I knew this Sitrick well, nay, loath'd him;
Yet caught by grandeur, gave my plighted faith:
Too late repentance wounds my tortur'd breast,
Too late I feel an unavailing flame,
And prove the torment of a vain desire.   [*Exit.*

End of ACT FIRST.

ACT

A C T II.

S C E N E, *Palace of* Dublin.

SITRICK, PHARON.

SITRICK.

DRAW near my faithful Pharon---ftill haft thou been
The partner of my counfels and my arms ;
And ever have I found thee as I hop'd,
True to thy truft, and loyal to thy prince.
Then know, that e'er this fun revolves its courfe,
The man whom Sitrick calls his greateft foe
Shall be no more---Ceallachan fhall die.---

PHARON.

Shall die !---forgive the amazement that I feel
At fuch a ftrange reverfe, and let me afk
What mean thefe gaudy preparations here,
That indicate the joyful bridal feaft ?
What meant the embaffy to Munfter's court,
That offer'd gentle peace to all its realm,
And beauteous Stira to its monarch's bed ?---

SITRICK.

Why, all was meant to make deftruction fure.
The wily ferpent, e'er he ftings, difplays
A thoufand beauties to delight the eye,
And tempt the unwary traveller's approach ;
Then quickly darts upon his certain prey :
Thus Munfter's king beholds fair Stira's charms,
Nor dreams that he advances to his fate.

PHARON.

PHARON.

But how accomplifh this thy purpos'd fcheme ?
The world proclaims the wifdom of thy foe ;
He fure requir'd fome hoftage of thy faith ;
Nor trufts his perfon, without ample proof
Of fafety to himfelf and to his train.

SITRICK.

Thou know'ft him not, nor doth the foolifh world;
It thinks him wife, I prove its judgment falfe---
No fooner did he fpy the gilded bait,
Than down it went, quick as my wifhes afk'd ;
Nor fhall he find the well difguifed hook,
Till Sitrick, like a fkilful angler, ftrike,
And undeceive him at the price of life.

PHARON.

But fay, my lord, from whence thy plan arofe ;
And how conducted ?---

SITRICK.

    ---Thou fhalt hear, my friend.---
—When laft---(perdition feize his conqu'ring arm)
When laft Ceallachan o'ercame my troops,
And drove me vanquifh'd from the bloody field ;
My wife, my fifter too, thou know'ft were ta'en,
And led in triumph to the Irifh court :
(But out of that fhall fpring my great revenge) ;
For there, the youthful monarch's amorous heart,
Open to love, receiv'd the piercing fhaft,
And Stira's beauty all his foul fubdu'd.---
Inform'd of this, I brought it to my aid,
And offer'd her the bond of future peace :
The lover fir'd with recollection ftrong

                    Of

Of all the graces of her lovely form,
Now haftens here, nor once demanded ought
To bind the treaty, or fecure himfelf.

PHARON.

Pardon, my Lord, the freedom of my tongue,
And hear thofe cooler thoughts thy welfare prompts---
Tho' much I wifh deftruction on thy foe ;
Yet muft I think, thy fafety will forbid
To execute what now thou haft propos'd :
Reflect on all thofe valiant dauntlefs tribes
Ceallachan commands ;---whofe meaneft troops
Would gladly forfeit life for dear revenge :
Then image to thyfelf, refentment rous'd
By fuch a deed ; and prudence muft declare
How fatal the attempt.---

SITRICK.

                    ---Prudence may paint
In ftrongeft lines each dreadful confequence ;
But, by yon heav'n he dies : my mad'ning foul
Now rages with revenge, which nought can cool
But his deftruction :---Let me but behold
His lifelefs corfe, and all his hofts may come.---

PHARON.

Since nought can change my prince's fix'd refolve,
Let caution dictate what thy vengeance claims :
Let him be made the captive of thy arms :
Then may'ft thou offer liberty and life,
On thefe conditions---that he'll ftraight yield up
Each place of ftrength and fortrefs in his fway.---
If he confents, his people's love is fuch,
That they will fure comply.---Then may we find

                                        Some

Some after-means to give the wifh'd-for death :
Thus fhall thy vengeance have its full demand,
And fafety be fecur'd.---

SITRICK.

     ---Thou counfel'ft well ;
It fhall be fo.---But hafte, my Pharon, hafte;
Lead forth a chofen band, and quickly gain
The rear of Munfter's train---fhould ought infpire
Ceallachan with doubt, or in his mind
Sufpicion raife, this will prevent retreat.

            [*Exit.*

Manet PHARON.

 The profpect brightens, fhe may yet be mine,
Nor honour, nor Cleones interpofe---
Ha ! what will Cleones fay, when he beholds
The faith of nations, and of men betray'd---
When he beholds, perhaps, a monarch's blood
To vengeance fhed, and fpilt by Pharon's aid ?---
Oh, no ! that muft not be---I'll watch with care,
Each confcious fting that pierces Sitrick's breaft,
Difplay the horrors that await remorfe,
And change the bloody purpofe of his foul. .. ..

            [*Exit.*

SCENE *changes to a woody Country near* Dublin.

Enter two IRISH OFFICERS *in converfation.*

1ft OFFICER.

'Tis ftrange indeed---Duncan to Dublin gone,
The King in thought wrap'd up---All is not right---

    D 2   2d OFFICER.

2d O F F I C E R.

May Heav'n avert whate'er difturbs his peace :
Sure he whofe ample foul delights in all
That tends to aid the meaneft of mankind,
Can ne'er deferve a pang.---

1ft O F F I C E R.

---None are exempt
From life's mis-haps---But where's Ceallachan?
Haft lately feen him ?

2d O F F I C E R.

---Yes,—e'en now we met ;
He enter'd yonder wood, whofe leafy top
A pleafing umbrage fpreads, that foothes the mind
Where contemplation reigns, and leads it on
To pour its feelings forth beneath thofe bow'rs,
Whofe filent fhade our confidence invites---
Behold where now he walks, clofe to yon oak,
With folded arms ;---with flow and thoughtful pace,
In awful meditation loft to all.

1ft O F F I C E R.

Let us retire, nor rudely interrupt
His folitary courfe---when thus inclin'd
For folitude and converfe with one's felf,
How irkfome even thofe whom moft we prize.

2d O F F I C E R.

The obfervation's juft---this way let's go ;
Nor feen by him, intrude upon his thoughts---

[*They go out on the oppofite fide, from that by
which* Ceallachan *enters.*

CEALLA-

CEALLACHAN *Solus.*

How ftrange is man!---his wifhes when obtain'd,
But fhow the fool he wants a fomething ftill---
Speed, fpeed, ye loitering moments of fufpence ;
No more diftract me with thy hopes and fears ;
Give me to know my fate, whate'er it be,
For dread of evil is the worft of ills.
But, lo ! my Duncan comes, and from his eye
The fparkling luftre fhoots forth heart-felt joy---

Enter DUNCAN.

Oh ! fpeak, my friend, and let thy words proclaim
What looks expreffive have already told.

DUNCAN.

Let joy unbounded reign throughout thy breaft ;
For know, my royal liege, the beauteous maid,
With modeft boldnefs owns a mutual flame---
" Go tell the generous prince you ferve," fhe faid,
" That every future blifs on him depends.
" Tell him, without a blufh, I own my love,
" And view with rapture the approaching hour
" That makes me ever his"---

CEALLACHAN.

---This, this is blifs ;
Thus to poffefs that moft fupreme delight,
The having pow'r to make my Stira blefs'd.
Now ev'ry gloomy view Defpair had bred,
But ferves to make the profpect pleafe the more.
O my friend, how can I e'er thy zeal repay
For tidings fuch as thefe !---

DUNCAN.

---I'm amply paid.
Wretched the man, whofe hard, unfeeling heart

Receives

Receives not pleafure from another's blifs :
But when my King, my friend, is happy made,
It then is ecftacy---

C E A L L A C H A N.

    ---I know it is,
To gen'rous fouls like thine. Thefe happy rites
Shall fheathe the deadly fteel ; our glitt'ring arms
No longer for deftruction us'd, fhall range
In pleafing order. o'er our peaceful walls,
And give their fplendor to the focial feaft.
Let other monarchs mad ambition boaft,
Whilft I purfue love's happier fcenes ;
Yield all my foul to its ecftatic blifs ;
Poffefs'd of Stira, court the peaceful fhade,
Nor idly wander in purfuit of fame.

D U N C A N.

 O flatter not thyfelf, my royal Lord ;
Neceffity will oft oblige thee to refume
Thy arms neglected, and the martial field ;
Will oft oblige thee to forfake the couch,
Where love's delicious raptures lull thy foul ;
For tranquil fcenes belong not to a throne.

C E A L L A C H A N.

 Think not thy monarch's fword fhall e'er be fheath'd,
When lawlefs infult calls its vengeance forth.
But ftill the moment of returning peace
Shall be embrac'd :---Still fhall my tend'reft care
Be then employ'd to heal Deftruction's wounds ;
Each peaceful art fhall then renew its toil,
And Induftry reflourifh o'er the land.

          D U N C A N·

D U N C A N.

Munſter, what happy days for thee's in ſtore;
Whoſe monarch thus, in all his ſchemes, purſues
His country's welfare and his people's good!

C E A L L A C H A N.

O rather ſpeak the happineſs of him,
To whom the indulgent hand of Fate hath giv'n
A pow'r to gain ſuch godlike ends as theſe.----
Is there a tranſport that this world can boaſt,
Equal to that which in the boſom glows,
When from the low'ring brow of wretchedneſs
You pluck its ſorrows, planting in their room
The chearful, glad'ning look, Content inſpires?
Oh! grant not merit to the only act
That pays me for the troubles of a throne.

D U N C A N.

E'en Nature form'd thee for a king, and gave
A ſoul exalted as the rank you bear.

C E A L L A C H A N.

You view me, Duncan, with a partial eye.
But come, my friend, the beauteous Stira calls,
And all a lover's wiſhes urge me hence.   [Exeunt.

SCENE *changes to a different Part of the Wood.*

Enter P H A R O N *and a* Daniſh Captain.

P H A R O N.

Thou ſeeſt where yonder hill its ſummit rears,
Whoſe ſpacious ſide's with branching oaks o'erſpread,
That hide in ſhade the ſtream that runs beneath---
                                    Thither

Thither extend the left, in silent march,
And as the Irish troop proceeds, advance :
Should you perceive the signal we've agreed,
With rapid pace thy gallant soldiers lead
To join with mine, and intercept the foe.
Thou to the post assign'd, and I to mine.   [*Exeunt.*

SCENE *changes again.*

CEALLACHAN, DUNCAN, *and the* IRISH TROOPS *re-enter.*

DUNCAN.

Trust me my liege, some treachery's on foot :
Amidst those distant trees, the Danish garb
This moment caught mine eye :---the clash of arms
I also heard, or else mine ears deceive :
Allow me to explore the neighbouring wood,
And see that safety on thy steps attend.

CEALLACHAN.

No dread of danger in my breast I feel.---
But come, my Duncan, satisfy thy doubts ;
Lead to the spot from whence these fears arise.

SCENE *changes.*

Enter PHARON *and* Danish CAPTAIN.

CAPTAIN.

This way they march, nor longer seek our walls :
A moment brings them up.---

PHARON.

PHARON.

　　　　　　---Then let us hafte
To ftop their purpos'd courfe; but ftrictly charge
Each valiant Dane to fpare the monarch's life ;---
For he who takes it, pays it with his own.　　[*Exeunt.*

S C E N E *changes.*

Enter C E A L L A C H A N, D U N C A N, *and the*
IRISH *Train.*

C E A L L A C H A N.

Ha! is every pafs befet ?---

D U N C A N.

　　　　　　---Each pafs is clos'd
With thronging Danes---one only choice remains,
To yield fubmiffion, or to part with life.---

C E A L L A C H A N.

Oh! for a thoufand of my Dalgais now !---
But fay, my gen'rous friends, how beats each heart ?
Doth glory nerve each valiant warriors' arm ?
Will ye ignobly live, or bravely die ?

A L L.

We fcorn ignoble life---we'll bravely die.---

C E A L L A C H A N *draws his fword.*

Then, thus I hurl defiance at the foe.
What are ten thoufand flaves oppos'd to men
Who fight for freedom, and for glory burn !
Let's on, my gallant youths, there is the path
　　　　　　　E　　　　　　　　　Thae

That leads to Munfter, to each focial tie :
Think what your country, what your fires demand ;
Think of a monarch's wrongs, and follow me. [*Exeunt.*

[*Fighting is heard for fome time behind the Scenes, af-
ter which* Ceallachan *and* Duncan *enter engaged
with* Pharon, *and a number of the* Danes.]

P H A R O N.

Yield up thy fword, nor urge deftruction on.---

C E A L L A C H A N.

Yes, flave, when life's no more,---

P H A R O N.

...What madnefs this !
To force like ours, what is thy ftrength oppos'd?---
Submit, and tafte our mercy.---

C E A L L A C H A N.

---Thy mercy, wretch !
Thus I revenge a monarch's wrongs---

D U N C A N.

...And thus---
[*Whilft they are rufhing on the enemy, a party
comes behind and difarms them.*]

C E A L L A C H A N.

Off! cowards off !---

D U N C A N.

---Unhand me, villains !---

P H A R O N.

PHARON.

Soldiers, your pris'ners guard with due refpect;
Our fcatter'd troops my care demands...

[*Exit.*

[*The* Danifh *Soldiers remain at a little diftance.*]

[Ceallachan *and* Duncan *come forward.*]

CEALLACHAN.

Oh, Duncan! I am fick at heart---behold
Thofe ftreams of blood, that lately flow'd for me---
Each valiant youth, who round me fought, hath paid
The tribute of his life, fave only you ;
Thou too art doom'd to meet a monfter's rage,
And to his vengeance bleed---All-gracious Heav'n
Heap forrows yet unheard-of on this head ;
But, oh ! in pity ceafe thefe cruel fhafts
That pierce me thro' the bofoms of my friends.

DUNCAN.

Let not one thought for me difturb thy mind ;
My friendfhip grew not by the foft'ring gales
That profperous fortune blows ; nor can the blafts
Of wint'ry ftorms, rais'd by adverfity,
Deftroy the hardy plant.---To die with thee ?
'Tis nought---have we not ftill fince earlieft youth,
Gone hand in hand ;---no feparate pleafures known ;
In joy, in grief, ftill equally partook ?
And would'ft thou then at laft fhake off thy friend ?

CEALLACHAN.

Let me embrace the noblcft of mankind.
Thus with the man whofe fad appearance fhows
A fhatter'd fortune and a clouded day ;
Whofe gay companions of his brighter hours,

Vanifh

Vaniſh with them, and leave him to his fate ;
If then a real friend appear, it chears.
His drooping ſoul, his value well he knows,
And clafps the kind conſoler to his breaſt.

PHARON *enters, and ſpeaks.*

PHARON.

Moſt valiant King, and you brave Sir, muſt ſtraight
To Dublin's walls proceed---Sitrick commands,
And his commands I muſt obey---

CEALLACHAN.

       ---I know
Thou art his ſlave, nor ſhall I talk to thee
Of broken faith, and nations' rights betray'd---
Lead on, we'll follow, Sir---O now, my friend,
Undaunted let us meet this final ſhock,
The laſt that mortals know---Tho' none have pow'r
To ſhove misfortune back, or change the courſe
By Heav'n's high will decreed ; yet all may riſe
· Superior to thoſe ills they can't prevent.
Hence, to that world we'll take our anxious flight,
Where ſacred Virtue only meets reward.

                      [*Exeunt.*

End of the SECOND ACT.

ACT III.

SCENE, *Palace.*

SITRICK *diſcovered in a Room of State, a* Captain *in waiting.*

SITRICK.

GO tell the gallant Pharon, that Sitrick burns
To thank his faithful zeal.----Bid him conduct
His priſ'ners here.----   [*Exit* Capt.
        ----My plan muſt now ſucceed---
This bar remov'd, my arms ſhall quick prevail
O'er all Hibernia's Chiefs :---her fertile plains
Shall own me for their lord, and all her wealth
Shall ſoon be mine.----But then the world condemns,
Deteſts the deed ; and brands my hated name
With ev'ry term that infamy can give.
Now conſcience too uplifts her awful head,
And in the midſt of all my triumphs
Stings my boſom with remorſe ;---deſtroys each joy,
And every ſcene diſturbs.---   (*a long pauſe.*)
        ---What---yield him up ?
Reſign, forego the advantage I have gain'd?---
Ambition and revenge forbid retreat,
And I obey.---Welcome, my faithful Pharon,

[PHARON *enters with* CEALLACHAN
DUNCAN, Danes, *&c.*]

Well

Well haſt thou fill'd the poſt to thee conſign'd,
Whate'er it fits me to beſtow, demand :
Thou ſhalt not aſk in vain.....

PHARON.

.....Thus to receive
My royal chief's applauſe, is great reward :
Yet Pharon's wiſhes would prefer a ſuit,
He fears might give offence.—

SITRICK.

—Speak freely then ;
For on my ſoul, ſo much I prize thy worth,
I know not ought I would to thee refuſe.

PHARON.

Embolden'd by this kindneſs of my lord,
Some fitter ſeaſon Pharon will preſume
To be thy ſuitor.—

SITRICK.

—Well then, be it ſo.—
At length, Ceallachan, our arms prevail ;
No more art thou victorious o'er the Danes ;
But now the priſ'ner of their conquering ſwords.—
Thou know'ſt what vengeance on thy head impells ;
Yet hear our mercy—If now thou wilt conſent
To what our terms require, thy liberty,
And Stira's hand, may ſtill be thine.—

(Ceallachan *gives a look of anger and contempt.*)

—Ha! what !
Doſt thou behold me with an eye of ſcorn?

Doſt

Doft thou not know my power? doft thou not know
That if I will, this moment is thy laft!—

(Ceallachan *repeats his look, and ftill remains filent.*)

Again! nor even deign to anfwer me?
By Heav'n I'll break thy fpirit, and teach thee, Prince,
Prefumption's due.—.

CEALLACHAN.

—Say'ft thou, prefumption's due?—
Tho' to hold converfe with a wretch like thee,
Is far beneath the man whofe actions flow
From the pure fountain of an honeft heart;
Yet will I ftoop to ftrike thee with difmay.
Soon fhall my valiant Dalgais, and the tribes
That fpread along the Shannon's fertile banks,
With fwords high brandifh'd tear thee from thy walls:
Soon fhall they give thee what thy deeds deferve;
Soon make thee an example to mankind;
That fear henceforth the villain may deter,
Where virtue binds not, and where honour fails.—

SITRICK.

Hafte, flaves, and bear this haughty monarch hence:
Let ev'ry keeneft torture be prepar'd
That art çan teach—when his disjointed limbs,
And mangled flefh in agony fhall writhe;
We'll fee if thus he'll brave our wrath.—

CEALLACHAN.

—Then learn
Inhuman Dane, fuch cruelty is vain:
Perhaps this feeble flefh may fail its lord;

May

May tremble on the rack, and own its pangs:
But the pure foul fhall glory in its truth ;
Shall rife exulting to its kindred fkies,
And look with horror on a ftate like thine.

SITRICK.

Hence—lead him to his fate—

PHARON.

—Let me intreat
A fhort delay—when rage to reafon yields,
He'll quick comply.—

SITRICK.

—Well then, at thy requeft
He fees to-morrow's dawn.....But know, proud king,
If at the rifing fun you fhould refufe,
That Waterford and Cafhell's lofty tow'rs,
That Corke and Limerick's ample walls, with all
The towns of ftrength in Munfter's wide domain,
Be inftant yielded to the Danifh fway ;
Thy life fhall glut my vengeance !—

CEALLACHAN.

—Such threats are idle,
When apply'd to me—for know, I fcorn a life
That's in thy pow'r to give or take away.—

SITRICK.

When all the dread array of Fate appears,
Then wilt thou beg, perhaps, may beg in vain,
Nor gain the boon you afk !—

CEAL.

CEALLACHAN.

     —Think'ſt thou my ſoul
So little knows the firmneſs of a man,
That poorly frighted by the trick of woe,
Shock'd by a mere parade, I could reſign,
A loyal nation to tyrannic ſway?
Had you e'er felt the flame of patriot fire,
Whoſe purifying blaze ennobles man,
And baniſhes each baſe, each ſelfiſh thought,
Far from the breaſt wherein it deigns to dwell,
You then would know a monarch's fix'd reſolve;
Would know, I court the terrors you diſplay,
And, for my country's welfare, long to die!

SITRICK.

'Tis greatly talk'd---but know, this ſingle day
Is thine. Conſider well, and think on life.

CEALLACHAN.

And think on life!---Each word degrades thee more,
And pity almoſt mingles with my rage.
But why thus talk to thee? where we deſpiſe,
Silence is the beſt reply.

SITRICK.

     Wilt thou ſtill dare
To brave our wrath? We'll try theſe boaſting words.
Haſte, my Pharon, with chains this hero bind;
Let coarſeſt food his hunger ſerve, nor let
One ray of light illume his diſmal cell.
In other walls let Duncan be confin'd.
Not e'en thy friend ſhall ſhare or ſooth thy woes;
Thou ſhalt be prov'd.
       F   CEAL-

CEALLACHAN.

---Come, and behold the proof---
Come, and behold me in the dungeon's gloom,
Superior to the ills that throng around;
And learn to value what thou can'st not know.
Then quickly lead me to the stroke of Fate;
With love of country throbbing at my heart
I'll meet the destin'd blow, and show thee, Sitrick,
My life was in thy pow'r, but not my honour.

[*Exeunt* Ceallachan, Duncan, Pharon, *Guards. &c.*

Manet S I T R I C K.

By Heav'n, to hear the vauntings of this man,
One would suppose he was the victor!

S T I R A *enters in great diforder, and kneels.*

S T I R A.

Oh, with a brother's eye behold me kneel,
Nor let a fifter's heart, with woe o'ercharg'd,
Burst from its feeble bounds, and rush to death.
If e'er our parents to thy mem'ry rise,
Who with their last, their latest breath bequeath'd
My helpless youth to Sitrick's care ! if e'er
You felt one spark of fond paternal love
Arising in thy breast ; oh! grant my pray'r---
Let Munster's King to freedom be restor'd,
And bless thy fifter with the man she loves.

S I T R I C K.

Away, thou stain to Sitrick and thy race !
How dar'st thou call our royal parents' shades

Te

To witnefs to thy fhame?—degen'rate wretch
To let thy country's foe engage thy heart,
And warm thy breaft to love!——I'll caft thee off,
Nor own thee of my blood——

S T I R A.

——Oh! think, my Lord,
And let thefe tears, this bleeding heart prevail.
'Twas you that rais'd my fond, expecting hopes,
To that delightful ftate where late they foar'd.
O do not then thus blaft each promis'd blifs,
Thus drive me to defpair!---

S I T R I C K.

---Thou wanton, ceafe---
Doft thou not blufh to own thy country's hate,
The object of thy bafe impetuous flame——
The man, of whom our babes with horror fpeak,
And weeping matrons curfe?——

S T I R A.

——Wrong me not thus,
Nor wound a wretched fifter's fpotlefs fame.
No wanton paffion in my bofom dwells,
No thought that veftals might not wifh to own.
If 'tis a crime to fee and to admire,
Where ev'ry gen'rous tender virtue joins
To form the man——I gladly boaft my guilt.

S I T R I C K.

If thus thy tongue wilt riot in the praife
Of Sitrick's foe, farewell. I'll hear no more——

[*STIRA holds him.*]

S T I R A.

Yet hear me, Sitrick, grant what I implore,
I will not aſk thee for theſe promis'd rites ;
Such wiſhes I'll reſign—All I requeſt
Is this——Reſtore him to his country's arms ;
Let him be free, and may you be moſt bleſs'd.
Not e'en my ſorrows ſhall diſturb thy peace :
The mourning Stira, from the world retir'd,
Shall ne'er intrude one ſigh t' offend thine ear.
Beneath ſome ſhade my tears ſhall harmleſs flow,
And o'er my cheeks in ſilence glide away,
Till in the grave thy ſiſter's griefs are laid,
And all is huſh'd within the peaceful tomb.

S I T R I C K.

Why wilt thou plead, to ſave a life he ſcorns?
The haughty monarch braves approaching fate :
My offer'd terms are treated with contempt !
E'en Stira's charms have loſt their wonted force,
Nor can they now ſubdue ſo cool a lover.——

S T I R A.

Alas ! had he, my Lord, but coolly lov'd,
He had not been by thee betray'd.——

S I T R I C K.

——In vain
You ſeek to change thy brother's fix'd reſolve :
My terms accepted, can alone reſtore
Ceallachan to liberty and thee.
Haſte then, employ perſuaſion's utmoſt art ;

With

With all that matchlefs beauty urge thy fuit,
Avert his ruin, and regain repofe.——

[*Exit.*

Enter BEDA, *as* SITRICK *goes out.*

BEDA.

O fay, my Stira, have thy tears prevail'd?
Have thy entreaties touch'd thy brother's foul?
O fay! is Munfter's monarch doom'd to die,
Or doth foft pity melt the tyrant's breaft,
And ward deftruction off?——

STIRA.

——Alas! my friend,
Still doubtful is his fate—if he confents
To Sitrick's terms, the hero yet is mine—
But, oh! thofe terms have been already tried,
Have been already treated with difdain.

BEDA.

O could you gain admittance to the King,
Perhaps all-powerful love might lend its aid,
Might change the firmnefs he fo lately fhow'd,
And raife up wifhes for a longer life.—

STIRA.

'Tis now my only hope—by Sitrick's will,
Thy Stira haftes to try this laft refource.
Oh! I will quickly feek the fuffering chief;
Ufe all the tender foftnefs of my fex,
Plead the fweet raptures that await on love,
Melt into tears, and fteal upon his heart:

Then,

Then, when I find him bending to my wishes,
Seize the fond moment, and obtain compliance. [*Exit.*

Manet BEDA.

Go, lovely maid, may angels wait your steps,
Inspire your tongue, and crown you with success.
No more I'll seek your nuptials to prevent,
No more to misery add the weight of guilt,
Nor be a rival, where I seem a friend.
How dreadful is a state of dark disguise,
When every word must studied be, before
It ventures forth—when every look is train'd,
And taught the guilty language of a lie?
Can the deceitful bosom ever know
A bliss like that which swells the noble heart,
Where conscious rectitude inspires each thought,
And proudly owns the dictates of the soul? [*Exit.*

SCENE *changes.*

Enter PHARON *and* CLEONES.

PHARON.

I seiz'd the fav'ring moment fortune gave,
And to the haughty Dane reveal'd my passion.
Beyond my hopes he list'ned to my suit,
Bade me expect his lovely sister's hand,
If at the rising of to-morrow's sun,
The monarch still reject his offer'd terms—

CLEONES.

My Lord, I would not willingly offend;
Permit me, therefore, to with-hold my thoughts.

I've

I've learn'd indeed for to reftrain my tongue,
But cannot utter what I do not feel.—

PHARON.

Nay, then you ftill remember my offence,
Nor haft thou yet forgiv'n my foolifh rafhnefs.—

CLEONES.

Believe me 'tis long fince forgot.—But fay,
Why fhould I wound the feelings of a friend,
And give a cenfure where he hopes applaufe?

PHARON.

O fpeak, my friend, as thou wert wont to do,
When in our boyifh days we firft efteem'd ;
When, from the joyous train of fportive youths
We chofe each other out ; together roam'd,
Together chac'd our rural hours away.
Think of that friendfhip we fo oft have vow'd,
Nor longer fear you can again offend.—

CLEONES.

Far different were thofe days which you recall;
Then the pure foul, untainted by mankind,
In native innocence ador'd its God,
Difplay'd the rich perfection Nature gave
In love with virtue, and of vice afraid.
Oh! Pharon, what a foe to man is man?
When, from the peaceful fhade of rural life,
They crowd together, corruption flows apace ;
Unheard-of crimes arife to curfe the world,
And punifh men, for violated laws.

PHA-

PHARON.

Happy indeed, our youthful moments pafs'd;
Yet fituation cannot change the foul:
Are we not ftill the fame fond friends, Cleones?
Or art thou alter'd, and to Pharon falfe?

CLEONES.

I am the fame, but thou art chang'd indeed!
Before thy mad ambition led thee on
To feek for glory in the Danifh court,
How would'ft thou Pharon, have beheld thofe deeds,
Which now thy ready hand can ftoop to aid?
How would'ft thou then have view'd a king betray'd?
One too, whom e'en the malice of a foe
Might feek to cenfure, and yet feek in vain.
Oh! in thofe hours of unpolluted life,
Methinks I now behold thy glorious rage;
Thy ready fteel almoft unfheath itfelf,
And as the treacherous tale was told, thy eyes
Flafh lightning from their orbs, whilft ev'ry nerve
Grew big with manly indignation!—

PHARON.

—Alas,
I feel the juft reproach:—Yet fure, my friend,
When for the public, ftratagem is us'd:
When policy requires a hidden act,
The very colour of the deed is chang'd;
And that, which in the private fphere of life
Abhorrence claims---then merits our applaufe.

CLEONES.

Oh, Heav'n! where will mankind's prefumption end?
When thus they dare to alter thy decrees,

To change thofe laws their great Creator fram'd,
And give to villainy the praife of virtue !
If the affaffin, for the price of blood,
Stab in the dark, and give the hired blow;
If from revenge the poniard be unfheath'd,
And buried in the heart for which 'tis drawn;
You call it murder; and as fuch you punifh:
But when the ftatefman acts beneath the mafk
Of feeming peace, and of fictitious treaty,
Till he with fafety can deftroy a foe;
Both wealth and honours crown the very act
For which a lefs exalted villain bleeds !

PHARON.

Chide on; chide on; for I have yet fo much
Of virtue left, as to admire Cleones.
O prove thyfelf a kind, a gen'rous friend ;
Point out the way by which I can regain
Thy loft efteem, and what is yet ftill more,
My own applaufe !—

CLEONES.

—O Pharon ! afk thyfelf;
For confcience is not dead within thy breaft :
Afk if Ceallachan deferves to die ;
Afk if the mourning Stira fhould be thine ;
Examine then the part which you have play'd,
And know the conduct you fhould now purfue.

PHARON.

Oh ! I will hafte, and try my utmoft fkill,
To fave the monarch's life, and fet him free;

G   But

But to refign the fond, the flatt'ring hope,
Of Stira's being mine, is furely more
Than even Virtue can demand.—

C L E O N E S.

—You dream!

Where is the hope I afk you to refign?
Doth not the lovely maid e'en now deplore
A captive lover and averted rites?
O hafte, my lord, a gen'rous paffion fhow,
With inborn greatnefs plead thy rival's claim :
Lead him to happinefs which can't be thine ;
Wipe from her eye the pearly drop of grief,
And prove at leaft that you deferve her love.—

P H A R O N.

Yes, then! my better angel, I will go;
Will drive this mift of paffion far away ;
No longer plunge impétuous into guilt,
But be again the partner of thy virtues.

[*Exit.*

Manet C L E O N E S.

May Heav'n fupport thee in the great refolve.
But, oh! I fear, like to the meteor's blaze,
'Twill for a moment fhine, and then expire.
When firft, untutor'd in the wiles of men,
In fweet fimplicity, I knew thee, Pharon,
Ne'er was a mind more richly grac'd than thine!
How could example then thus change thy foul?
But what cannot example do? at firft
The ingenuous mind with horror views

The

The frightful form of vice.—But foon, alas!
The dire contagion fpreads.——We dare to do
What we but lately fhudder'd to behold.
Each finer feeling is by cuftom drown'd;
We catch the reigning manners of the age,
And lofe abhorrence for the worft of crimes.

                               [*Exit.*

End of the THIRD ACT.

ACT

ACT IV.

CEALLACHAN *discover'd in Prison,*
with a single Taper burning.

[*Comes forward.*]

CEALLACHAN.

WHERE now the regal pomp and proud parade?
    Where now my thronging chiefs, eager to show
A real or fictitious zeal? and, oh! where now
The nuptial torch, and Hymen's blissful rites?
The radiant sun ne'er shed his golden beams
Around a happier monarch's brow, when last
His bright effulgence bless'd the world:
But thus the fabric moulders into dust,
Whose base is founded on the ground of life.
Ah! foolish man, who to the future blind,
By Fancy's gay creation fondly paints
Sweet scenes of bliss that never can arrive:
Each passing day the lov'd delusion proves;
Yet ev'ry day brings forth some new deception.

  [*Turns, and sees* STIRA *at the bottom of the Stage.*]

Ha! doth some bright phantom mock a wretch?
Or can it be?—It is, it must be she:
For she alone's possess'd of such a form!—

              [*Runs to her.*

Oh! thou bright maid, who thus benignly shines,
                     Amidst

Amidft furrounding gloom; Oh! quickly fay,
Doth that foft bofom beat indeed for me?
Do thofe fad tears from mutual paffion flow,
And is the bloody Sitrick only falfe?

STIRA.

O think not hardly of thy Stira's faith!
No bafe deceit this bofom e'er hath known;
By Sitrick's art I too have been deceiv'd,
No brighter profpect e'er a maid beguil'd:
To plunge her from tranfporting look'd-for blifs,
To all the matchlefs horrors of defpair.

CEALLACHAN.

Oh! thou art truth itfelf,—in every look
I read the rich perfection of thy foul.
Oh! let me wipe thofe courfing tears away;
Let me infold thee in thefe longing arms,
Gaze on thy beauty, prefs thofe balmy lips,
Till loft in raptures of ceftatic blifs,
I tafte of heav'nly joys before I die.

STIRA.

Yet live, my lord, to love and me—if no more
Of pow'r depriv'd, to Munfter you'd return,
With thee to fome lone rural fpot I'll fly,
Sequefter'd from the world, with thee be blefs'd,
Nor think of royalty refign'd.—

CEALLACHAN.

                    .—Oh! no:
Tho' my foul pants for fuch a ftate with thee,
A thoufand reafons do my blifs obftruct,
And place eternal obftacles between.

                              STIRA.

STIRA.

What, tho' glory may not on the deed attend ;
Yet love its balmieſt influence ſhall ſhed,
Shall make us happieſt of the human race.
No pomp I ſeek, no glittering badge of power,
No ſplendid roof, no high repaſt demand ;
So thou art mine, I care not for ſuch toys.
With thee the humbleſt cot will ſtill delight ;
The ſimpleſt food, the coarſeſt dreſs will pleaſe :
With thee the pleaſing partner of each toil,
Theſe hands ſhall gladly labour, from the morn
Till in the weſt the evening ſun deſcends ;
Then by thy friendly arm upheld, I'll ſeek
The peaceful ſhelter of our ſweet retreat ;
There welcome in the night with vows of love,
And bury ev'ry care within thy arms.

CEALLACHAN.

Ah ! ceaſe ; ſuch unexampled love refrain :
Already doth my reſolution ſhake ;
To liſten longer would my fall complete.
Had Fortune plac'd me in an humbler ſphere,
How eagerly I'd ſeek ſome rural ſpot,
Far from the noiſe and buſtle of the world,
By woods emburied, and by rocks begirt :
There would I taſte true happineſs with thee ;
With thee, each ecſtacy of love enjoy ;
And bleſs the lowly lot whoſe peaceful toil
Ne'er led me from my Stira's charms away !
But now, my honour and my fame's at ſtake ;
Nay more, my love ; for love like thine muſt ceaſe,
When it no longer can eſteem.—

STIRA.

S T I R A.

—Ah, talk not thus—

What is this honour, or this bubble fame,
Whose airy praise, thus tempts us to forego
All real, for imaginary blifs?—

C E A L L A C H A N.

What else but these could keep mankind in awe?
Virtue and vice in one dark chaos hurl'd,
No bright reward would spur the hero on;
No infamy the villain would deter.
But say, doth Stira wish me to comply?
Would she embrace the king, whose selfish soul
Could meanly practice on a people's love?
Could thus affassinate the public weal!

S T I R A.

'Gainst thee and virtue, I no longer plead.
O never, never quit thy glorious course!
—To yield our darling private passions up,
When public good the sacrifice requires;
Is this world's bounds t' o'erleap—aspires to heav'n,
And treads upon the footsteps of a God.—

C E A L L A C H A N.

Thou heav'nly maid, for ever could I hear
Those accents sweet, which flowing from thy tongue,
Appear to be divine. Would but the fair
Thus plead in Honour's cause; would beauty thus
Our kind instructor prove; degraded vice
Would hang abash'd, and seek its native gloom:
Benevolence, with pure unspotted love,
Would then dispense their heav'nly joys around,
And with angelic blifs inspire mankind.

Enter

Enter Captain *to* STIRA.

CAPTAIN.

Madam, the royal Sitrick quick demands
Thy prefence.—

STIRA.

—Go, fay I fhall attend his will.

[*Exit* Capt.

And fhall we never, never meet again !
Is all my promis'd blifs for ever fled !
Is this to be the laft fad fcene of love !

CEALLACHAN.

O ftop thofe tears, they pierce me to the foul!
Terrors unknown now rife within my breaft,
Shake my refolves, and make a coward of me !
To part with life I nothing deem'd : but, oh !
To part with thee is more than I can bear !

STIRA.

Methinks I now behold thy mangled corfe—
Thy body writhing in the pangs of death !—
O fave me, fave me from the direful image !
The dread idea fires my heated brain,
And madnefs will enfue!—

[*She throws herfelf on his bofom.*

CEALLACHAN.

—Oh ! my lov'd Stira,
Yield not to fuch thoughts !---the pitying Heav'ns,
Who now behold our innocence and woes,
May yet, by fome unlook'd-for means avert
Impending ruin, and our blifs reftore.

STIRA.

STIRA.

Vain is the hope---no pitying Heav'ns avert
Thy haplefs fate : too furely wilt thou bleed ;
And, oh! diftracting thought, wilt bleed for me!

Enter CAPTAIN *again.*

CAPTAIN.

Thy royal brother fends once more, to bid
Thy inftant prefence.---

STIRA.

---Retire, I'll follow thee.

[*Exit* Capt.

CEALLACHAN, *embraces her.*

And muft we part? muft I refign thee then?
Oh! Stira, for ever could I hold thee thus;
Here clafp thee, till the hand of drooping age
No more obey'd the dictates of the foul :
E'en then, my clofing eyes fhould look on thee,
My fault'ring tongue pronounce thy darling name,
And the laft finking pulfe fhould beat with love.

STIRA.

O let me go, whilft yet 'tis in my pow'r!
My lips deny an utt'rance to my thoughts.
Oh! let thefe tears fupply the place of words,
And bid to thee, my lord, a fad farewell.—

[*Goes flowly out.*—Ceallachan *gazes after her—then*
fpeaks.]

CEALLACHAN, *Solus.*

Thus doth the wretch whom fome o'erwhelming wave
Hath fwept from off the deck, behold the fhip

H   Pafs

Pafs rapid thro' the deep—ftill as fhe goes,
His hopes of life decline ; no longer feen,
Defpair o'erpow'rs his foul ; he ftrives no more,
But yields, without a ftruggle, to his fate.   [*Exit.*

SCENE *changes to the Palace.*

Enter SITRICK *and* PHARON.

SITRICK.

What then, doth Pharon plead in fuch a caufe ?
Seeks he to loofe a lion from the toils,
Inflam'd by infult, and with vengeance fir'd ?
No, by the manes of my royal fire,
He yields fubmiffion to the Danifh arms,
Becomes a tributary vaffal to our fway,
Or falls a victim to his ftubborn honour.

PHARON.

O think, my lord, whilft yet to think is thine ;
Nor let ill-grounded fears miflead thy foul.
Gen'rous and noble is the captive king,
Above the paffions of a vulgar mind :
Give but thy lovely fifter to his arms,
Let liberty unpinion'd wait his fteps,
Not clogg'd with bafe conceffions ; and truft me, Sitrick,
You'll gain a friend, where you fufpect a foe.

SITRICK.

Ha! do I wake ? is Stira held fo cheap,
That Pharon flights what he fo late implor'd?
Doth Sitrick ftoop to join his blood to thine,

That

That thou fhould'ft fcorn the bounteous gift; fhould'ft
    praife
With lavifh tongue the man I hate, and prove
Ungrateful to the hand that rais'd thee?

PHARON.

—————My Lord,
Is this ungrateful, when thus thy Pharon pleads
'Gainft all his fondeft wifhes could demand?
When thus for Sitrick's welfare he'd refign
Far more than life—the woman he adores?
O do not wrong thy fervant's faithful zeal,
Nor wound a bofom that would bleed for thee!

SITRICK.

Forgive th' impetuous temper of thy Lord,
And know that he no longer doubts thy truth.
—But, lo! the mourning Stira hither comes,
And in the fettl'd fadnefs of her brow,
I read the haughty monarch's ftern refolve.

STIRA enters.

What then! hath female foftnefs urg'd in vain
Its fond attachment and the joys of love?
Could he unmov'd behold thofe ftreaming eyes,
Nor by compliance chace thy tears away?
Now by the immortal gods! if yet one drop
Of Denmark's royal blood courfe thro' thy veins,
And tell thee of thy birth, thou'lt be reveng'd!
Wilt to a fonder lover give thy hand,
E'en in the prefence of this haughty king;
And greatly fhow, you've learn't to fcorn the man
Whofe pride's fuperior to his love for thee!

       STIRA.

S T I R A.

Could he to felfifh pleafures yield up all
That fpeaks the monarch, and adorns the man,
He would indeed deferve my fcorn.   For know,
Tho' Stira feels each weaknefs of her fex;
Tho' unavailing woe muft caft a fhade
O'er every future hour; and grief unceafing,
Thro' a fad exiftence, wait me to the grave;
By all the powers of Heav'n I fwear,
I'd rather bear it all, than give my hand
Where forfeit honour was the price that gain'd it!

S I T R I C K.

No more fhalt thou abufe thy brother's patience
With idle nonfenfe and romantic folly.
Entreaties from this moment ceafe; and now
In me thou feeft a mafter, whofe pow'r fupreme
Muft be confefs'd————Madam, behold the man
Whom Sitrick deftines for thy lord——and learn
That my commands henceforth fhall be obey'd.

P H A R O N.

I'm loft again, and virtue is no more.
                                            [*Afide.*

S T I R A.

Doth Sitrick know fo little of my foul,
That thus he deals forth threats to fhake my truth?
Think'ft thou the maid Ceallachan prefers,
Can ever ftoop to own another Lord?
No!   By that royal blood which fills my veins,
Which lifts my fex fuperior to its fears,
If death alone can fave my plighted faith,
In death I'll fhow thee what it is to love!

                                            Enter

Enter a DANISH CAPTAIN *to* SITRICK.

CAPTAIN.

My Lord, my Lord, the Irish chief is gone !
By wond'rous means he————

SITRICK.

————Ha ! Ceallachan efcap'd !————
Bring forth the treacherous guard————

CAPTAIN.

————My royal Lord,
Duncan alone hath from thy troops efcap'd :
His garb forfaken, and a bar remov'd
Declare the wondrous means by which the chief
Obtain'd a paffage to the waves below.
Th' aftonifh'd Danes e'en yet their fenfes doubt,
So daring was the act ; and all agree
He perifh'd e'er he reach'd the foaming deep,
Or in the raging billows met his fate.

SITRICK.

'Tis well : I'm calm again.   Double the guard
That watches o'er the eaftern tow'r, and fee
That future vigilance for this atone.

[*Exit* Captain.

Nay then, fince bars, fince waves oppofe in vain,
My tardy vengeance fhall no longer fleep.
Madam, prepare my pleafure to fulfil :
For know, e'er yet the moon's reflected light
Doth for the wearied fun illume the heav'ns,
The holy prieft fhalt give thee to my friend,

Whilft

Whilft Munfter's King beholds the facred rites,
And learns to dread that power he now contemns.
Nay, fpare thy tears; they on a lover fail'd;
And truft me, Stira, will not now. avail.

[*Exit* Sitrick.

PHARON.

Permit me, beauteous maid, to foothe thy woes,
And fhare at leaft the grief I cannot cure.
If to adore thee more than all thy fex;
If to have lov'd in filence from that hour,
When firft thofe heav'nly beauties caught mine eye,
Can merit a return, 'tis Pharon's right.
O let me then thus feize thy hand——Thus fpeak...

STIRA.

Away...thou bafe infulter go,---nor prove,
That every virtue hath forfook thy breaft!
My forrows would be private, Sir——not feen
By fuch as thou art!————

PHARON.

————O kill not with thy fcorn,
The man who loves thee; to diftraction loves----
But give thy pity, if thou giv'ft no more.

STIRA.

O Heav'ns! doft thou prefume to talk of love?
Love is the produce of a generous foil,
Shoots forth luxuriant in the noble mind,
Is nurs'd by virtue, and by honour fed.
It fprings not in the tainted heart,
Nor dwells in fouls like thine.————

PHA-

PHARON.

————Oh! wrong me not.
Could'ſt thou behold the feelings of this heart,
No longer would theſe keen reproaches flow.

STIRA.

Thy *virtues* are indeed to me unknown.
Unleſs the blood of innocence betray'd,
Unleſs ſubſervience to a tyrant's will,
Be rank'd as ſuch—but hear me e'er I go :
Not all the power of him thou calleſt lord,
Shall ever force me to be thine---for know,
That death is welcome, when compar'd to thee.

[*Exit.*

Manet PHARON.

ˮ Is death then welcome, when compar'd with me ?
No, no ; when paſſion ceaſes, other thoughts
Will fill thy breaſt, and life again be priz'd.
Tho' now the object of thy hate, the hand of time
Will change thy ſoul, and make me dear to thee.---
With kind attention, and unceaſing love
I'll melt thy ſtubborn heart---and make thee own
That Pharon merits————

CLEONES *enters.*

————Ha ! Cleones here !—
I dare not meet his eye. Let me withdraw,
Nor ſeem to have perceiv'd that he approach'd.

[*Exit.*

CLEONES *Solus.*

My Lord—Cleones would addreſs thine ear—
He ſhuns me then, and thus declares his vow
Forgotten,

Forgotten, and his purpose chang'd—In vain
I've fought to call extinguifh'd virtue forth;
In vain have fought to fave this godlike King.—
Oh, what a ftate is mine? my grateful foul
Bound to Ceallachan by ties moft ftrong,
Now fees the hour of fate draw near, without
A ray of hope.—Oh, thou Almighty Power,
Supreme of Heav'n! an humble fuppliant hear—
Grant me the means this hero to preferve;
Give me to pay the mighty debt I owe him,
And in his ftead let me to vengeance bleed.

[*Exit.*

End of the F O U R T H   A C T.

A C T V.

S C E N E, *Palace of* Dublin.

S T I R A, B E D A.

S T I R A.

THE hour of fate draws near—the chiefs are met,
  The holy prieft prepares the folemn rites,
Waits but a nod th' Almighty to blafpheme,
And give a fanction to the worft of crimes.
O fay, then, Beda, is thy friend forgot?

B E D A.

O no, my Stira, I have been too true,
Nor broke a promife I fo rafhly made.

                              [*Shows a Phial.*

Behold the dreadful gift that friendfhip brings.

S T I R A, *fnatches the Phial.*

Thus let me feize the precious draught, and blefs
The bounteous hand from whence it came.

ATTENDANT *enters to* STIRA.

A T T E N D A N T.

Thy royal brother with impatience waits
Till you appear—for you alone delay
Th' expected rites, and univerfal joy.

I

S T I R A.

STIRA.

Go tell thy mafter, Stira comes—and comes
Prepar'd for thefe expected rites.—Away—

[*Exit* Attendant.

Yes, Sitrick, this fhall free me from thy power;
This fhall preferve from violation's hand,
And fhow the wondering world how Stira lov'd.—

[*Drinks.*

'Tis done—No nuptial torch fhall now difplay,
The wretched victim of a brother's will.
But in its ftead, the funeral taper fhall
Diffufe its fickly beams around my corfe,
And add frefh horror to the difmal fcene.
O what a change is this! But come, my friend,
We will obey the fummons of thy Lord—

[*Exeunt.*

S C E N E *changes to a Room of State,*
difcovering Sitrick, Pharon, Prieft, Danes,
&c.   Cleones *thoughtful, and feparate*
from the reft.

S I T R I C K, *to an Attendant.*

Once more require the princefs to attend.
Go fay that Sitrick and that Pharon waits;
And fee that prompt compliance doth enfue.

[*Exit* Attendant.

[*To* C L E O N E S.]

And thou, Cleones, bring the captive king.
Firft fhall this haughty monarch own our fway,

Then

Then fhall he—

     [A great noife is heard.

 —Ha! what ftrange alarm thus ftrikes our ear—
Thus rends the vaulted roof with martial founds,
Of diftant war ?—

    Enter CAPTAIN.

    CAPTAIN.

   ——To arms ! to arms ! my Lord,
Nor lofe a moment—Already are our walls
Afcended by the foe—With dreadful fury
On they rufh, and every tongue cries Vengeance···
Each his fellow urges on, and fhouts
" Our King we'll free, his horrid wrongs revenge,
" Or perifh all."———

    SITRICK.

  —Ha ! the troops of Munfter here !
This inftant fhall their monarch die :—take this—

    [Gives a Signet to Cleones.

Bury thy poniard in his heart, and fay,
'Twas Sitrick fent thee :—away !—

     [Exit Cleones.

  — Now to the fight
We'll lead our valiant Danes ; with fury meet,
And drive thefe rafh invaders from our walls.

     [Exeunt.

SCENE *changes to the Prifon.*

GEALLACHAN *difcover'd fleeping on the Ground—*
CLEONES *enters and gazes on the* King.

CLEONES.

Happy the man whofe uncorrupted foul
No guilty deed difturbs :—calm and ferene,
Amidft impending ills, he lives in peace—
Stretch'd on the earth is blefs'd with gentle flumbers,
Which fplendid roofs, and beds of fofteft down
Oft court in vain.—But, lo ! the prince awakes.—

CEALLACHAN, *(rifing).*

Speak—what fecret purpofe brings thee to thefe walls?

CLEONES, *fhewing Signet and Poniard.*

See this, and this, brave prince, and guefs the reft.

CEALLACHAN.

I guefs it all, and am prepar'd to die.—
Thou feem'ft difturb'd; humanity calls forth
Thy pity for my fate, and ftops thy arm !—
Fear not to ftrike the blow—'tis Sitrick's act ;
And all the guilt belongs to him.—

CLEONES.

　　　　　　　　　—View me :
This face examine well—recollect'ft thou ought
That tells thee we have met before ?—

CEALLACHAN,

　　　　　　　　—Thou art
To me unknown ;—nor can I recollect,
That e'er I faw thee till this hour.—

CLEONES.

CLEONES.

　　　　　　　　　　—Then, thus
I execute a tyrant's fell command.

[Throws away the Dagger, and unbinds him.

Haft thou forgot that day, when funk to earth
I begg'd for life, nor did in vain implore?—
Thy fword uplifted, ready to defcend,
Fell harmlefs to the ground;—Thy boon be thine,
Thou cried'ft; if e'er a foe beneath thy arm
Shall fink, fpare thou his life, and I'm repaid.—
Oft have I wifh'd fome blefs'd occafion fince,
This debt to pay, and thus 'tis now difcharg'd.
Thy troops now ftorm the fouthern fide ;—take this.—

　　　　　　　[Gives Ceallachan *a fword.*

Thefe walls no longer thee detain.—For me,
I'll hafte to where the thickeft fight prevails ;
There in my country's caufe provoke my fate !
This act forbids me to furvive.—

　　　　　　　　[Exit Cleones.

Manet CEALLACHAN.

　　　　　　　—He's gone !
O may fome guardian power his purpofe thwart,
And fave him from himfelf !—Is't poffible !
My troops already here !—How can it be !—
But now's no time for thought—This way leads forth.

　　　　　　　　　　[Exit.

SCENE

SCENE changes to SITRICK's Palace.

Enter DUNCAN, IRISH OFFICERS, Soldiers, &c.

DUNCAN.

No tidings of our monarch yet?—Thofe gates
Thrown wide, which late the King confin'd, declare
Some dreadful deed.   O! fhould he be no more,
What joy can vict'ry yield, or conqueft give ?
Let's hafte and learn his fate, whate'er it be :—
But, hark ! fome one with hafty ftep draws near :—

CEALLACHAN *enters.*

'Tis he !—he lives !—and all my fears are o'er.—

CEALLACHAN.

Come to my arms, my lov'd, my gallant friend :
Words are too poor to fpeak thy prince's thanks.—
And ye my brave, my faithful warriors all
Accept th' o'erflowings of thy monarch's heart ;
Whofe grateful foul fhall well repay thy love,
But never can forget it.—

ALL.

—For fuch a king,
Who would not fight? who would not die ?—

CEALLACHAN.

—Once more
I thank ye all :—now Duncan let me know,
By what unlook'd-for means I fee thee here !—

DUNCAN.

DUNCAN.

Then briefly thus :—Beneath night's friendly shade
I gain'd the waves that wash'd my prison's base,
And reach'd the shore without these hostile gates.
Not many hours had I pursu'd my way,
When to the right, amidst the trees I spy'd
The glare of arms ;—the moon's full orb display'd
The forms of men, and the quick ear bespoke
Approaching steps :—alarm'd, I chang'd my course,
And to the left prepar'd to fly :—just then,
A party rushing forth oppos'd my way :
But, what my glad surprize ! when I beheld
These dear companions of my earliest arms :
My father led them on : from him I learn'd,
Some few had scap'd unnotic'd from the fight,
Had reach'd his camp, and told the treach'rous deed :
Enrag'd he march'd th' impatient troops,
And thus unlook'd-for are we here.—

CEALLACHAN.

      — But say,
How was the victory gain'd ?—I burn to know
The glorious fight ;—Haste, let me hear it all.—

DUNCAN.

Fir'd by my tale, we quickly reach'd these walls,
And led our furious troops against the foe :
The Danes surpris'd, at first made no defence ;
We gain'd the wall, and beat their feeble guard :
But soon the day was chang'd ; their swarming troops
Clos'd up each gap of death, and seem'd t' increase,
Not lessen by our slaught'ring swords :—in vain
Our little band oppos'd their dauntless breasts,

         To

To all the fhock of war : Their numerous foes
With unremitting fury drove them on,
To where a dreadful precipice o'erhangs
The briny wave ; defpair fill'd ev'ry heart,
And certain death appear'd on ev'ry hand :
When, lo ! the valiant Fingal, ever firft
Bright glory's path to tread, on Sitrick rufh'd,
And grafp'd the tyrant in his dreadful arms !
Vengeance, he cry'd ! and with a furious fpring,
From off the rock he leap'd ! another chief
Th' aftonifh'd Pharon feiz'd with equal rage,
And copied Fingal's god-like deed !—The Danes
A moment ftood, and fearful gaz'd below.
Such defperate acts their fortitude fubdu'd ;
Such defperate acts our troops infpir'd ;—They fled,
And conqueft crown'd our arms.—

CEALLACHAN.

        —O glorious men !
Such deaths as yours make even conqueft dear.
But fuch men do not die !—their deeds immortal,
Borne on the wings of time, for ever live ;
For ever claim the tribute of applaufe !
Eternal honours wait their facred fhades,
And from their afhes future heroes fpring !

DUNCAN.

My royal liege, among the captive Danes
One chief was ta'en, who feem'd to court his fate ;—
Ne'er did thefe eyes behold a braver warrior.—

CEALLACHAN.

Ha ! conduct him hither.

                [*Exit* Duncan.
                Mean

       —Mean time, my friends,
Let no rude noife difturb this facred roof.
Far be the din of arms remov'd from hence ;
Nor let one hoftile deed proclaim us victors ;
For here my Stira dwells. I'll feek her ftraight,
And foothe her troubled fpirits into reft.

          [*Exit.*

 [CEALLACHAN *goes out on one fide, Soldiers*
 - *on the other.*]

SCENE *opens, difcovering* STIRA *ftretch'd
on a Couch, as if dead* ; *Attendants weeping
round her.*

   Enter CEALLACHAN.

 What mean thefe founds of woe ?—Celeftial pow'rs!
Do I behold my Stira thus !—

        [*Kneels by her.*
    —Oh! lovely maid,
Here will I gaze, here ftay while life remains !
O look on me as thou wert wont, and glance
That foft delicious fondnefs to my foul :
O let thofe balmy lips once more pour forth
Harmonious numbers to my ravifh'd ears.
Alas ! thofe eyes have loft their melting fweets ;
Thofe lips no more their heav'nly founds difpenfe ;—
Death revels over every charm !—
Hark !—fhe calls !—fhe chides my loitering hand !—
    [*He ftarts up, and draws his fword.*
I come! I come! and thus—

   [BEDA *runs in, and feizes his Arm.*

    K   BEDA.

BEDA.

——This rashness cease;
And learn from me, that Stira yet survives:
By me deceiv'd, no poison hath she ta'en,
But in its stead a draught of wond'rous pow'r,
Which for a time each sense doth lull to rest,
As if th' infranchis'd soul had bid adieu
To its frail dwelling.——

CEALLACHAN.

——Do not trifle with despair;
But as you hope for happiness to come,
Tell me if this strange tale doth bear the stamp
Of holy truth!——

BEDA, *pulls out a Phial.*

——This shall answer all thy doubts:——
                    [*Applies it to* STIRA.
Behold! the lily yields its sickly hue,
And the rich streams of life renew their course.——

CEALLACHAN.

She breathes!——her eye resumes its wonted lustre,
And the pale cheek regains its blooming honours.——
                    [*Turns to* BEDA.
Yes! my guardian angel, she doth survive!
Yet shall my charmer live and make me bless'd.

STIRA *raises herself, and looks wildly round.*

Surrounding spirits, say! what mansion this,
Where Stira's doom'd to dwell!——methinks these walls
Are not unknown!——My lov'd attendants too!
Sure that is Beda! and, oh! thou lov'd shade,
                    [*To* Ceallachan.
                                        Is

Is Heav'n indeed thus kind, to give me thee?—

CEALLACHAN.

My lovely fair, recall thy wand'ring fpirits;
Thou haft not yet thy debt to nature paid:
No deadly poifon tears my Stira hence;
But years of blifs fhall crown thy virtues here!

BEDA.

Forgive a fraud by friendfhip prompted, and live
A happinefs to tafte, unknown to me.
I'll bid the world adieu; and now devote
The remnant of my days to holy deeds.
Farewell.—Oppofe me not—nor vainly feek
To change the fettl'd purpofe of my foul.

[Exit Beda.

STIRA.

Since thus refolv'd, O may that peace be thine
Which holy deeds deferve!—And now my Lord,
O tell me, where is Sitrick?—Whatever crimes
His foul debafe, he is my brother.—

CEALLACHAN.

—Alas!
He lives no more.—

STIRA.

And by thy arm he fell?

CEALLACHAN.

O no! my love;—this hand could ne'er have fhed
Thy brother's blood:—Before I join'd my troops,
Th' unhappy Dane from Fingal met his fate.

K 2

Nay,

Nay, weep not thus; but fay, thou beauteous maid,
When may I hope—

S T I R A.

—Oh! talk not now of love!—
Already doft thou know, how dear thou art.
When Stira ought to give her hand—on you,
And you alone, fhe will beftow it.—

C E A L L A C H A N.

—Enough.
Forgive a lover's ardour; and know, my fair;
Thefe nicer feelings do the more endear thee.—

DUNCAN *enters, with* CLEONES *in Chains.*

D U N C A N.

Behold, my liege, the Dane, whofe furious arm—

CEALLACHAN *runs to* CLEONES.

And do I fee my kind deliverer thus!—

                    [*Turns to Soldiers.*
Unloofe thefe chains—to him ye owe your king!

                    [*They take his chains off.*
Say, gen'rous Dane, what can a monarch give,
That worth like yours, wilt honour with acceptance?

C L E O N E S.

Moft noble king, one only boon I afk—
Let not the Danes to juft refentment fall:
Forget thofe wrongs, which but difgrac'd thy foes;
And having conquer'd them, thyfelf fubdue.

                              C E A L.

CEALLACHAN.

Such worth as thine for all thofe wrongs atone.—
No power I claim o'er Denmark's fons, fave that
Of making thee their Lord.—

CLEONES.

          —With grateful thanks,
Permit me to decline this purpos'd rank ;—
It fuits not with the man—

CEALLACHAN.

          —Urge not too far
This nicenefs of thy foul : none can demand
A fuller proof of moft exalted worth :
Thou'rt form'd to rule ; nor will I be denied.
          [Turns to DUNCAN.
Go loofe the chains of ev'ry captive Dane ;
Banifh their fears, and tell them they are free :
Then fee, my Duncan, that our valiant troops
Elated with fuccefs, opprefs them not ;
Nor bafely give an infult to the fall'n.

(Addreffes the Audience.)

When in the field we meet oppofing foes ;
When fteel to fteel is clos'd in deadly ftrife,
Let Rage infpire, and Fury ftalk at large :
But when the fortune of the day is caft ;
When in the vanquifh'd we no longer meet
Contending arms—let Mercy walk abroad,
The conquer'd foothe, and mitigate their pain ;
The dying comfort, and the wounded heal.
Succefs indeed our admiration draws ;
But 'tis Humanity deferves applaufe.

E P I L O G U E.

By the AUTHOR.

Spoken in the Character of STIRA.

NAY, *stop that rising grin—I come not here,*
    To raise a laugh, or wound the modest ear.
No wedding-jest ; nay, not one double phrase,
Shall make the timid blush, or wanton please.

  Tho' fix'd by custom, that some comic strain
Should soothe your woes, and mitigate your pain ;
Our bard presumes to wear a solemn face ;
To quit the beaten path of sly grimace :
Gives the shrill notes of laughter to the wind,
And to reflection leaves the feeling mind.

  Ye Fair, attend ! like me still faithful prove,
Yet first, like me, with caution fix your love.
Let no soft nonsense steal upon the heart ;
Be not the captives of each coxcomb's art :
But when with honour manly sense unites,
And the fond lover all your love invites ;
With freedom own—nay, glory in the flame,
And think unshaken truth your noblest fame.

  Ye gen'rous Youths, this godlike hero view,
His virtues copy, to his worth prove true.
When war's dread clangor gives the loud alarm,
Let fury nerve each daring warrior's arm :

                                                 But,

But, in these hours of soft endearing peace,
Let horrid rage and civil discord cease :
No more unsheath the ornamental sword,
Nor combat for a rash unguarded word.

Somewhat there was the Poet bade me say,
To deprecate your wrath, and save his play.
Oh—'twas to tell you 'tis his first offence—
But be not trick'd by any such pretence ;
For, tho' I dare not speak—'twixt you and I,
He ne'er again will at your mercy lie.

THE END.

www.ingramcontent.com/pod-product-compliance
Lightning Source LLC
Chambersburg PA
CBHW022143090426
42742CB00010B/1375